# MORE TRUE STORIES FOR CHILDREN

Translated by

**Matina Wali Muhammad**

Published by

**Ta-Ha Publishers Ltd.**
**1, Wynne Road**
**London SW9 0BB**

Published by
**Ta-Ha Publishers Ltd.**
1 Wynne Road
London SW9 0BB
website:http://www.taha.co.uk/
email: sales@taha.co.uk



General Editor: Afsar Siddiqqui
Translated by: Matina W. Muhammad
Edited by: Ahmed Thomson
Illustrated by: M. Ishaq

British Library Cataloguing in Publication Data
Muhammad, Matina Wali
More True Stories for Children
I. Title

ISBN 1 897940 02-5

Typesetting by JL &GA Wheatley Design, Aldershot. Tel: (0252) 212998

Printed and bound in Great Britain by
Deluxe Printers, Park Royal, London NW10 7NR
**email: deluxeprinters@aol.com**

# CONTENTS

# 1
# EID MUBARAK

It was the day of the Eid, a day of great rejoicing and celebration. There was an air of festivity in the streets of Madinah with all the people, both young and old, dressed in their best clothes. Many of the children were wearing new clothes which they had been given especially for that day.

As the time for the Eid prayer approached, everyone made their way to the place of prayer, which was an open piece of land on the outskirts of the city. The Prophet Muhammad, *salla'llahu alayhi wa sallam*, arrived and led the prayer while the morning was still cool. After the prayer was over, he spoke to the assembled people, his words filling their hearts with fresh knowledge and understanding.

When he had finished, the people walked back into the city to eat in each other's houses, the little children running and playing here and there in excitement, smiling and laughing as they played, without a care in the world.

As he walked back, the Prophet, *salla'llahu alayhi wa sallam*, was suddenly aware of a little boy sitting by himself on the side of the path. The little boy was crying and looked very sad and sorrowful. The Prophet bent down and patted him on the shoulders.

"Why are you crying?" he asked.

"Please just leave me alone," sobbed the little boy, without even looking up to see who was talking to him.

The Prophet ran his fingers through the boy's hair and very gently and kindly asked him again why he was crying. This time the boy answered his question, although he still did not look up:

"My father was martyred fighting *fi sabili'llah*, and now that my mother has married again, my stepfather does not want me to live at home any more. Today is the Eid and everyone is happy. All the children have new clothes and nice things to eat, but I don't have any clothes except what I am wearing, and I have no food, and I don't even have somewhere to live."

Tears of compassion came to the Prophet's eyes, but he smiled and said, "I know how you feel. When I was a little boy I lost both my father and my mother."

The boy was surprised to hear that it was an orphan who was comforting him, and for the first time he looked up to see who it was. To his great surprise and joy, he saw that it was the Prophet Muhammad, *salla'llahu alayhi wa sallam*, and he immediately jumped to his feet out of love and respect.

"If I were to become your new father, and Ayesha your new mother, and Fatima your new sister," said the Prophet with a big smile, "would that make you feel a little bit better?"

"Oh yes!" said the little boy, smiling through his tears, "that would be the best thing in the world!"

The Prophet, *salla'llahu alayhi wa sallam*, took the little boy's hand in his and took him back home.

"This is our new son," he said to Ayesha, *radia'llahu anha*, who gave the boy's tear-stained face a good wipe before bathing him and then dressing him in new clothes. After giving him a tasty meal, she patted him playfully on the back and pointed outside:

"Now you can go and play with the other children," she said.

When the other children saw him, they were amazed to see how he had changed. They crowded around him, asking what had happened. After he had explained about the kindness of the Prophet, *salla'llahu alayhi wa sallam*, one of the children said to the others:

"If your parents had died, then Muhammad, *salla'llahu alayhi wa sallam*, would have helped you too, just as he helped this boy."

## 2
# THE BEDOUIN'S PROMISE

During the time of the second *khalif*, *sayyedina* Umar, *radia'llahu anhu*, a young Arab bedouin from a far off land was crossing the Arabian desert on his camel. After a long hard morning's ride, he came upon an oasis, and after watering his camel, he tied it to a shady palm tree and lay down in the shade of another one to rest while the day was at its hottest.

While he was asleep, the rope with which he had tethered his camel to the date palm came undone, and the camel slowly moved off in search of food. It had not gone very far when it came across a small garden, filled with tender young shoots and tasty leaves.

The owner of the garden, who was an old man, saw the camel eating his plants and threw a stone at it to frighten it away. However the stone hit the camel on the head and it died on the spot.

When the young man awoke, he discovered that his camel had gone and he went looking for it. He soon found the dead camel, and when the old man came up to him to tell him what had happened, he was so angry that he hit the old man before he had a chance to explain. Unfortunately his blow killed the old man.

The young bedouin was very shocked by what he had done and waited for someone to come, so that he could explain what had happened. After a while the old man's son arrived, and after being told what had occurred, he took the young bedouin before the *khalif* Umar, *radia' llahu anhu*. Since the young bedouin admitted to killing the old man, *sayyedina* Umar ordered that he be killed.

Now the young man owed a Jew some money, so he asked the *khalif's* permission to return to his town so that he could settle his debt before the death sentence was inflicted on him. *Sayyedina* Umar agreed that it was better if the debt were first repaid, but said that he could only release the young bedouin provided that someone agreed to stand surety for him while he was away.

The young man looked at the faces of all the people who were present, but there was no one there who knew him and who would be prepared to guarantee that he would return. He had come from a far off place, and all his friends were a long way away.

Seeing the disappointed look on the young bedouin's face, and recognising his honesty, Abu Dharr al-Ghiffair, *radia'llahu anhu*, who was one of the Prophet Muhammad's closest companions, *salla'llahu alayhi wa sallam*, stepped forward and said:

"I will stand as surety for him."

"Are you sure?" replied *sayyedina* Umar, "for if this young man does not return, then you will receive his punishment on his behalf."

"I am sure," said Abu Dharr. "I believe that I can trust him."

عيد مبارك

After thanking Abu Dharr for his generosity and promising him that he would indeed return, the young bedouin set out on the long journey home.

Time passed, and the day by which the young bedouin had promised to return arrived. Several people thought that the young bedouin had betrayed Abu Dharr's trust and that he had been deceived. As the deadline approached, they believed that it would be poor Abu Dharr who would be put to death. Abu Dharr, however, remained calm and unperturbed. Even when the appointed time came for the executioner to lift his sword, Abu Dharr remained certain that the young bedouin would not let him down.

At that very moment, someone in the crowd shouted out, "Wait! Someone is coming!".

At the *khalif's* command, the executioner paused and lowered his sword. Out in the desert, beyond the limits of the city, a cloud of dust heralded a galloping horseman, and after a while the young bedouin came racing up to the expectant crowd, pulling his exhausted horse to a halt in a flurry of sand.

"*Al-hamdulillahi wa shukrulillah!*" he panted. "Thank God I'm not too late! My debt has been repaid, thanks to the generosity of Abu Dharr, and now I am ready to receive my punishment."

*Sayyedina* Umar and everyone else who was present were impressed by the young bedouin's sincerity, but there was nothing the *khalif* could personally do to reduce his punishment. The *hudood* of Allah were clear and could not be ignored.

Suddenly the son of the old man who had been killed by the young bedouin's angry blow stepped forward and lifted his hand:

"I and my father's relatives forgive this young man for killing our father. There is no need for him to pay with his life, and we do not wish him to pay us any blood-money either. Let him go free."

So saying, he took the young bedouin's hand and shook it firmly. As the two young men embraced each other, *sayyedina* Umar, *radia'llahu anhu*, and the other onlookers smiled with relief. It was the best of outcomes and justice had been done:

"Allahu Akbar!" they shouted. "Allahu Akbar! Allahu Akbar!"

There are many lessons that can be learnt from this story:

The first is never to do anything in a hurry; think about it calmly before you act.

The second is to avoid wrong action; but if you do a wrong action, then do not try to hide it, because Allah already knows about it, and your recording angels have already recorded it.

The third is to keep your word, even if it means that you will have to lose your property or your life as a result; if you keep your promise to others, then Allah will keep His promise to you.

The fourth is to show mercy; show mercy to others, so that Allah will show mercy to you.

The fifth is to make sure that all your debts are repaid before you die; if a person dies while he or she is in debt, then his or her relatives or friends should repay these debts on his or her behalf; but it is better to leave this world as you came into it, possessing neither more nor less than nothing!

# 3
# THE WATERS OF THE NILE

The river Nile is the largest river in North Africa and one of the most famous rivers in the world. The Prophet Muhammad, *salla'llahu alayhi wa sallam*, once said that it is one of the rivers of the Garden. Without the waters of the Nile, many of the people in Egypt and Sudan would go hungry and thirsty, for it is these waters that irrigate their lands.

In the olden days, long before the time of the Prophet Muhammad, *salla'llahu alayhi wa sallam*, the people had a strange custom: Each year, at the height of the dry season, when the waters of the Nile were especially low, they would choose a beautiful young maiden and dress her in lovely clothes and sparkling jewellery. Then they would throw her into the river as a sacrifice, hoping that this would please the river and make its waters rise. The young maiden, who usually drowned or was eaten by crocodiles, was called 'the bride of the Nile'.

After the Muslims came to Egypt, things changed:

When *sayyedina* Umar was the *khalif*, he appointed Amr ibn al-As as the governor of Cairo. When the next dry season came, a delegation of people came to Amr ibn al-As and explained what their custom had always been, so as to ensure that the waters of the Nile would be replenished.

"Please let us choose the bride of the Nile for this year," they asked, "or else the waters may not rise and all our crops will be destroyed."

"This custom of your forefathers is both cruel and ignorant," replied the governor. "I forbid you to kill even one more young maiden in this way. You should be patient and see what Allah decrees."

After they had left, Amr ibn al-As wrote a letter to the *khalif*, explaining the custom, saying what he had done about it, and asking if there was anything else that he should do. On receiving the governor's letter, Umar Faruq wrote two letters, one to the river Nile and one to Amr ibn al-As.

The letter to the river Nile said: "This letter is from the slave of Allah, Umar ibn al-Khattab, to the river Nile. O river, if you flow only by the command of Allah, then we ask Allah only that your water continues to flow — and if you flow by virtue of your own power, then we do not need you!"

The letter to Amr ibn al-As instructed him to bury the letter to the river Nile in a dried up part of the river-bed.

Amr ibn al-As did as he was told, and soon after he had buried the letter to the river Nile in a dried up part of its river-bed, its waters began to rise — and they have never gone dry since then!

# 4
# HOW TO MAKE A LARGE PROFIT

During the time when *sayyedina* Umar Faruq was the *khalif* of the Muslims, there came a year when no rain fell. As a result the crops failed and famine gripped the land. The *khalif* told the people that if they held firmly to the *deen* of Allah and relied only on Allah, then they would survive the famine and it would pass. Nevertheless, it was a difficult and testing time for everyone.

It was during this time that a caravan of camels coming from the north came to Madinah. The camels were laden with food and merchandise, and whoever bought them from the leader of the caravan would be able to re-sell them at any price he liked, because the people would pay anything just to have some food in their stomachs again.

As it happened, *sayyedina* Uthman came to know of the caravan's existence before it had arrived in Madinah. He quickly rode out to meet its leader and bought the whole caravan from him for a handsome price.

When the news spread that *sayyedina* Uthman had purchased the entire caravan, all of the merchants of Madinah came to him, hoping to buy some of its contents. They offered him a high price, because they knew they could re-sell whatever they bought at an even higher price. However, whatever price they offered to give him for his merchandise was repeatedly refused:

"I want to make a large profit," he kept on saying. "I

have received a much better offer than what you are offering. I'm sorry, but no deal!"

No matter how high the price they offered, *sayyedina* Uthman's reply remained the same. Even when the *khalif* Umar went to him, his reply remained the same.

Everyone was very puzzled. Who was the mystery trader who had given *sayyedina* Uthman such a high offer? It couldn't be anyone from Madinah, because all the traders in Madinah had been turned down by him. How could *sayyedina* Uthman, who was usually so generous to the poor and needy, be so mean to the people of Madinah, especially now that they were really in great need? It really was unlike him to make money out of people in this way.

While everyone was thinking these thoughts, *sayyedina* Uthman led the caravan to the centre of Madina and called all the people to come:

"I told you that I wanted to make a large profit," he said, "and that whatever you offered, I had a received a better offer than that. Well, although some of you offered me the possibility of making a very handsome profit, no one has been able to match the offer made by Allah, for He has said, may He be Glorified and Exalted, that whoever gives away something in the Name of Allah will receive at least ten times as much as that, or even more, from Allah in return in this world, as well as being rewarded in the next world.

"No one else has made anything like such a generous offer as that. So I give this whole caravan to the people of Madinah, in the Name of Allah. *Bismillah*! Please share it fairly between yourselves!"

It was because of his great generosity, in the Name of Allah, that *sayyedina* Uthman became very rich. The more generous he was to others, the more generous Allah was to him. After the death of *sayyedina* Umar, *sayyedina* Uthman became the next *khalif* of the Muslims. He continued to spend out generously from what Allah had given him, in the way of Allah, until he was martyred. Since those who are killed in the way of Allah go straight to the Garden, this was his greatest profit of all.

# 5

# SAYYEDINA ALI'S JUSTICE

There were once two bedouins who were travelling together. One of them had five loaves of bread, and the other had three. They stopped under the shade of a large tree to have a rest, and were just about to have their lunch when they were joined by another traveller, whom they invited to share their food. They were all hungry, and between them they finished the eight loaves of bread.

When they had finished eating, the traveller who had joined the other two was so grateful that he gave them eight *dirhams* to share between them to pay for the bread that he had eaten. After the traveller had gone, the two bedouins could not agree as to how the money should be divided.

The man who had contributed five loaves to the meal said that he should have five *dirhams* while his companion should have three *dirhams*. The man who had contributed three loaves to the meal said that they should have four *dirhams* each.

Rather than argue about it, they decided to go and ask *sayyedina* Ali, *radia'llahu anhu*, to settle the matter for them. Having listened to their story *sayyedina* Ali said to the man who had contributed three loaves, "If you agree to what your companion thinks is fair, then you will be better off."

"No," replied the man, "I want *you* to decide this matter."

"Very well," answered *sayyedina* Ali, "I will give you my judgement. Do you agree that the three of you ate more or less the same amount of bread at the meal?"

"Yes, we did have equal shares," the two men replied.

"Right," said *sayyedina* Ali, "in that case, if you imagine each loaf being divided into three pieces, then with eight loaves that makes twenty-four pieces of bread altogether. At the meal each one of you had eight pieces each. Now the man with three loaves started off with nine pieces, and the man with five loaves started off with fifteen pieces.

"That means that the man with three loaves had eight pieces of his own bread himself, and only gave one piece to the traveller. The man with five loaves had eight pieces of his own bread himself, and gave seven pieces to the traveller. This means that the man with three loaves should have one *dirham*, and the man with five loaves should have the other seven *dirhams*."

The man who had contributed three loaves to the meal was very disappointed, but he could not help agreeing with *sayyedina* Ali.

"If only I had accepted *sayyedina* Ali's initial advice," he thought, "then at least I would have had three *dirhams*!"

# 6
# AS-SALAAMU-ALAIKUM

Love grows between people when they greet each other with the best of greetings: "*As-salaamu-alaikum*" : "*Wa alaikum as-salaam*" — which means: "*Peace be on you*" : "*And on you be Peace*".

The son of *sayyedina* Umar, Abdullah, *radia'llahu anhum*, knew this very well. He had noticed how the Prophet Muhammad, *salla'llahu alayhi wa sallam*, used to greet everyone with this greeting, whether they were young or old, rich or poor; and he knew how much all the Muslims loved their Messenger. Even when he came across little children playing about in the streets, the Prophet would always be the first to say, "*As-salaamu-alaikum*".

Accordingly Abdullah ibn Umar, *radia'llahu anhu*, tried to do the same. Wherever he went, he would nearly always be the first to say, "*As-salaamu-alaikum*". Sometimes he would go to the market place just to greet people. "*As-salaamu-alaikum*", he would say to everyone whom he met there, whether they were the merchants, or the shoppers, or the beggars, or even the travellers who were just passing through.

One day a man stopped him and asked, "Why do you keep on coming to the market when you hardly ever ask about the price of anything, or buy anything, or stop anywhere?"

"I just come here to say '*As-salaamu-alaikum*' to

everyone," smiled Abdullah ibn Umar. "That is much more important than any of the things that you have just mentioned!"

Abdullah ibn Umar, *radia'llahu anhu*, loved the Prophet so much that he tried to copy everything that the Prophet did, may the blessings and peace of Allah be on him, and on his family, and on his companions, and on all who follow him and them, with sincerity, in what they are able, until the Last Day. Amin.

**As-salaamu-alaikum!**